Trump

Trump

Alain Badiou

polity

First published in German as *Trump. Amerikas Wahl* © Passagen Verlag, Ges.m.b.H, Vienna, 2017.
English-language edition published by arrangement with Eulama Lit. Ag.

This English edition © Polity Press, 2019

Polity Press
65 Bridge Street
Cambridge CB2 1UR, UK

Polity Press
101 Station Landing
Suite 300
Medford, MA 02155, USA

ISBN-13: 978-1-5095-3607-8
ISBN-13: 978-1-5095-3608-5 (pb)

A catalogue record for this book is available from the British Library.

Library of Congress Cataloging-in-Publication Data
Names: Badiou, Alain, author.
Title: Trump / Alain Badiou.
Description: Cambridge, UK ; Medford, MA : Polity, 2019. | Includes
  bibliographical references and index.
Identifiers: LCCN 2018046813 (print) | LCCN 2018060069 (ebook) | ISBN
  9781509536092 (Epub) | ISBN 9781509536078 (hardback) | ISBN 9781509536085
  (paperback)
Subjects: LCSH: Presidents--United States--Election--2016. | Trump, Donald,
  1946- | Capitalism--Political aspects. | Elite (Social
  sciences)--Political activity. | Political sociology. | BISAC: POLITICAL
  SCIENCE / General.
Classification: LCC JK526 2016 (ebook) | LCC JK526 2016 .B34 2019 (print) |
  DDC 324.973/0932--dc23
LC record available at https://lccn.loc.gov/2018046813

Typeset in 12.5 on 15 pt Adobe Garamond by Servis Filmsetting Ltd, Stockport, Cheshire
Printed and bound in Great Britain by CPI Group (UK) Ltd, Croydon

For further information on Polity, visit our website: politybooks.com

Contents

Publisher's Note

The two lectures published in this book were originally delivered in English. The first was given by Badiou at the University of California, Los Angeles, on 9 November 2016, and was subsequently reworked by the author and delivered in French; the version here is based on the French text. The second lecture was given by Badiou at Tufts University in Boston on 17 November 2016.

Two Days after the Election of Trump

*University of California, Los Angeles**

Coming to speak to you this evening, and thinking about yesterday, about last night, when we
learned the results of the presidential election,
about Trump's success, I have had in mind a
beautiful line of poetry by Racine: "It was during
the horror of a deep night." Perhaps Racine was
contemplating the future, the election of Trump,
which, little by little, as the hours passed, became
undeniable, turning the depths of the election
night into something horrible. And under these
circumstances I recognized an obligation to speak
to you about the horrible thing that has just

---

* This lecture was translated from the French by Joseph
Litvak.

I

happened in the deep California night, for this counter-event, this disaster, makes it impossible for me to stand here before you all this evening and speak to you about this thing, however interesting it may be, in purely academic terms. You are distressed, stricken, appalled, and I must take as my point of departure what happened yesterday throughout the course of the deep night.

As you might imagine, what happened was, for me, as for almost everyone, a sort of surprise, a bad surprise, and the overwhelming consequence at first was the triumph of affects: depression, fear, panic, etc. But philosophy teaches us that none of these affects is in any way a good response, for they instead testify and even pay tribute, negatively and from our side, to the victory of the enemy. We must therefore think beyond these inevitable affects, beyond fear, disappointment, and depression. We must reflect on the political situation today, the situation of our world, and respond rationally to a question that is indeed urgent and haunting: what must the contemporary world be such that last night could have turned into such a horror? How is it possible for someone like Trump to be elected president of the greatest power in the world, the United

States of America? So my goal this evening is to present, if not a complete explanation, at least a clarification of the possibility of this distressing fact, as well as to propose, to submit for your discussion, certain thoughts as to how we must confront what happened in the deep, horrible night – what we must do that would not be subject to the law of negative affects but that would take place on the level of thought, action, and political resoluteness.

I am going to begin with a very general overview, not of the situation in the United States but of the situation in the world as we know it today. What is our world, in which the election of Trump, but also other extremely negative and horrible facts, can come about?

I think we must start with the most obvious point, but also the most important one: the victory, on a worldwide scale, of global capitalism. It is on this point, first of all, that we must insist. Since the 1980s – in other words, for forty years or so – we have been witnessing the historic victory of global capitalism.

There are several obvious reasons for this victory. The most important, of course, is the complete failure of the great socialist states, first

Russia, then China, and, more generally, the disappearance almost everywhere of the collectivist vision of the economy and of social laws, even in the form of a simple program. This disappearance extends even into the realm of theory, indeed of philosophy: today, Marxism is everywhere regarded as a thing of the past, as a relic of thoughts and conflicts that are no longer ours. The time is very distant in which Sartre could still declare that Marxism was "the untranscendable horizon of our culture." In fact, Marxism is now considered the very epitome of a transcended ideology. And this point is not in the least secondary, for it means that the situation of the world today, since the 1980s, is that of a major change, not only of objective reality but also of active subjectivities.

For more than two centuries, from the French *philosophes* of the eighteenth century to the great "leftist" movements of the 1960s and 1970s, public opinion was divided between two opposite ways of thinking about the destiny of humanity. At first, there was the opposition between the republican vision of the state and monarchical despotism. But then it turned into the opposition between the liberal doctrine of the free market on the one hand and the different varieties of social-ism and communism on the other.

For liberalism in the classic sense, private property is the key factor in the organization of society – at the price of enormous inequalities, to be sure, but, in liberal thought, everything has its price. On the opposite side is the socialist or communist or, indeed, even anarchist path, in the most abstract sense, according to which the end of inequalities must be the fundamental goal of human political activity – the end of inequali-ties, even if it requires a violent revolution.

We thus have on one side the supposedly peace-ful, legal, constitutional vision of the indefinite continuation of something very old, going back to the Neolithic age, namely the organization of all wealth and of the entire means of produc-tion under the legal form of private property, protected by the police and their power, and conceived of as the very heart of social life and of humanity. And, on the other side, we have the conviction, going back to certain aspects of the French Revolution, according to which the continuity of humanity's historical existence, at least since the Neolithic revolution, must allow for a second fundamental break, by rejecting the domination of private property and, consequently, by doing away with inequalities, thanks to a collectivized organization of production and exchange.

So, for two centuries, we had something like a strategic choice concerning not merely the facts and decisions of local politics, national obligations, wars and confrontations of all sorts, but indeed the general orientation, the historical future of humanity as a whole. For forty years or so now, our situation seems to have been the disappearance of this type of choice. Today the dominant idea is that there is no global choice – that, as Margaret Thatcher used to repeat, "There is no alternative" (by implication, to free-market capitalism). Which is to say that there is only one way, only one path for the future of humanity.

We must note that even Thatcher herself didn't say that this free-market capitalism to which there is no alternative, along with the monstrous inequalities that it entails, is perfect, or even very good. That wasn't her concern. All that matters is that it is the *only* solution. And that we must replace what the Chinese communists, in the time of Mao, called "the two-line struggle" – that is, the struggle between communism and

6

capitalism – with a *mandatory* consensus imposed by the real existence of only one way.

Contemporary propaganda in favor of liberal capitalism is by no means required to say that it is excellent, that it responds to all the material and intellectual needs of humanity. It is too obvious that this is false. Everybody knows it; everybody understands that the perpetuation of inequalities engendered by capitalism, and especially by the law of the concentration of capital, can hardly be a worthy destiny for human beings. Sartre used to say that, if the human species were capable of no more than that, it would leave no better memory of itself than that left by ants. "Perhaps," replies the liberal, dominant today. "But it's the only real possibility: everything else is both worse and ultimately impossible. Look at Russia, look at China." The power of the liberal capitalist way lies in declaring itself to be the only way. It doesn't even need to declare itself to be the best way, since it has succeeded in convincing practically everybody that another way, a second way, doesn't exist. Ants we may be, perhaps, but better to be an ant than nothing.

We can thus define the current moment as that of the imposition of the belief that liberal capitalism, which dominates virtually every country in the world, is the only possible destiny for human beings. And, in the process, we also get a definition of the human subject. What is a human subject in this ruling liberal vision? A human subject is an owner; if he isn't an owner, he had better be a salaried employee; in any case, he must be a consumer; and, if he is none of the above, he is nothing at all.

Now, what are the political effects of all this? What are the political consequences of this dominant vision of the world, which lays down the law that there exists only one strategic path for humanity as a whole? Every government, at any rate, must agree that this is the case. In today's world you cannot be tolerated very long as a head of state if you do not accept the dominant vision, that of the one and only path. No government anywhere in the world can say otherwise, lest it cause a crisis that will be its undoing. This is true of the recent "socialist" government in France, of the power of the "Communist" Party in China, as well as of the German or British government, of the powers in place in India or Japan, or of the president of the United States, whether Obama, Clinton, or Trump. All of them are saying the same thing: global capitalism is the only path that will permit the continuing existence of the human species.

In fact, I think that, today, any political decision, at the level of the state, depends strictly on what I would call a monster, namely global capitalism, with its inequalities, its crises, and its wars. It is not true that a government, today, can be an autonomous entity. From the very outset, it is tied down within an all-encompassing determination, and it must affirm that what it does, and even more what it *can* do, depends upon its adhering to the laws of this determination, which are the laws of the monster.

And the monster becomes more monstrous every day. For we have seen that, in the last forty years, the effects of the fundamental law of the concentration of capital have become extraordinary in the true sense of the term. After all, we must recognize that, today, 264 people possess as much wealth, in inheritance and income, as the 7 billion others who make up the rest of the world! This is a far greater imbalance than was possible during the age of absolute monarchies. There is in fact more inequality in the contemporary world than at any other period in human history.

And the fundamental law of the monster in question is scientifically defined – this is the heart of Marxism – not by more and more freedom but, rather, by more and more inequality.

Today, the role of the state is the same everywhere: to protect these inequalities, to protect the monster. Whether we are speaking of the French socialist government, the conservative German government, the Chinese Communist Party, the power of Putin in Russia, the colonial state of Israel, the Islamic state in Syria, or, of course, the president of the United States, all of them have only one maxim: keep a place, large or small, within the deployment of the monster – be or become a respected player in the international frenzy of the marketplace. With the result that, gradually, the whole political oligarchy, the whole political class, ends up constituting one single group – a group of people who are divided only by their competition for the best jobs but who have the same idea of humanity's destiny. The great traditional oppositions – Republicans versus Democrats, right versus left, conservatives versus socialists – become purely abstract, tied to a bygone era, for these supposed divisions rest on the same conviction, the same political and economic basis. All these divisions are traversed, undermined, and finally annulled by the fact, recognized by every politician and by every government, that, as far as the future of humanity is concerned, there exists one and only one path, that of global capitalism.

What is happening now is that this political oligarchy is being weakened in the Western world, because it is little by little losing control over the capitalist machine. By definition, global capitalism doesn't worry about its disastrous effects in this or that country. The contemporary bourgeoisie is to a great extent global: it is as comfortable in Shanghai as in Chicago, Berlin, or São Paulo. But, in general, politicians, for their part, operate at the national level, even as they depend largely on the fate of multinational corporations. Thanks to grave crises, false promises, and inappropriate "solutions," governments create among their people, on a large scale, frustration, misunderstanding, anxiety, and vague revolts. These negative affects among the people challenge, although in a very anarchic and confused manner, the one and only path – that of the monster – which, with only a few tiny differences, all members of the political class of today support.

In today's world, the exercise of politics is about these tiny differences, all inside the same global orientation. But this global totality has effects on the various peoples, effects of disorientation. Nobody can conceive clearly what a life with a meaningful direction might look like or what would be a strategic vision of the future of humanity. And, in this situation, a considerable part of humanity is seeking answers among false novelties, irrational visions, or a return to dead traditions. So that, opposite the traditional political oligarchy, we have the appearance of a new kind of activist, who defends violent and demagogic proposals and who seems more and more to take as his model gangsters or mafias, rather than trained bourgeois politicians. We have had this style of new politician in France, with Sarkozy and his gang. We have seen it in Italy, with Berlusconi and his mafia. We have it here, since yesterday, with Trump, the vulgar and incoherent billionaire.

It is often said that these new political figures – Trump, to be sure, but many others in the world today – resemble the fascists of the 1930s. There is indeed a certain resemblance. But, alas, there is also a major difference: today's new political figures do not have to confront the powerful and intractable enemies who were the Soviet Union and the communist parties. In fact, we could speak of these new figures in terms of a kind of "democratic fascism," a paradoxical but effective designation. After all, the Berlusconis, the Sarkozys, the Le Pens, the Trumps, are operating inside the democratic apparatus, with its elections, its oppositions, its scandals, etc. But, within this apparatus, they are playing a different score, another music. This is certainly the case with Trump, who is racist, a male chauvinist, violent – all of which are fascist tendencies – but who, in addition, displays a contempt for logic and rationality and a muffled hatred of intellectuals. The music proper to this type of democratic fascism is a discourse that does not worry in the least bit about coherence, a discourse of impulse, comfortable with a few nighttime tweets, and that imposes a sort of dislocation of language, positively flaunting its ability to say everything and its opposite. For these new political figures, the aim of language is no longer to explain anything or to defend a point of view in an articulate manner. Its aim is to produce affects, which are used to create a fleetingly powerful unity, largely artificial but capable of being exploited in the moment.

In Trump, we find once again the deliberate vulgarity, the pathological relation to women, and the calculated exercise of the right to say publicly things that are unacceptable to a large portion of humanity today that we also see in Hungary with Orbán, in India, or in the Philippines, as well as in Poland or in Erdoğan's Turkey.

Everywhere in the world, then, we witness this democratic fascism, which is internal to the parliamentary practices of modern capitalist "democracy," but which also produces an effect of artificial novelty, a different language, a violent false promise, and in some sense an external interior, something that is certainly within the bounds of the single path proposed by all the governments of the world, but set to a musical score in a manner different from that offered by the classical politicians hailing from the cultivated bourgeoisie. In this way, Trump and his kind produce, within the consensus concerning global capitalism, a spurious effect of novelty. He is like the hallucinatory harbinger of a "new path," all the while staying firmly within the path of the dominant oligarchy, whether cultivated or not. Trump is positioned so that, for a moment, he can say that there is something new, namely "Trump," the name and the thing, whereas what he is saying, in its particulars, which are nationalistic, sexist, racist, and violently pro-private property, is anything but new.

We thus find ourselves in a time when the oldest things in the world – such as the return, on one hand, to the deadliest and most ghastly religious traditions and, on the other, to primitive colonial capitalism in all its slave-masterly arrogance and boorishness – can seem like novelties, because they are forgotten modulations of the one and only path, whose inevitability must be imposed on us. In a sense, democratic fascism is nothing more than yet another artificial conversion of old things into novelties.

* * *

Let us proceed to a more systematic synthesis. I would say that we find ourselves inside an inevitable dialectic with four terms.

1 First, there is the complete brutality, the blind violence, of capitalism today. Of course, here, in the West, and particularly in old Europe, we

see only the secondary effects of this violence. But if you are in Africa, in the Middle East, in Asia, or in South America, you see it. And even here we witness capitalism's gradual return to what constitutes its true essence, namely the cult of "success" on the backs of others, the growth of inequalities, the dismantling of measures for social protection, the savage combat of everyone against everyone in a struggle to conquer a dominant position. This is the first term.

2 Then we have the decomposition of the classical political oligarchy, the end of the existence of a cultivated dominant class, and the appearance of what I have called "democratic fascism." Certainly, we do not know the future of this phenomenon. What is the future of Trump? In many respects, we do not know. And Trump probably does not know his own destiny. This was already quite obvious on the night of his victory. There was the self-satisfied Trump of the electoral campaign before the victory, and then there is the Trump who has gained power, and who seems somewhat frightened. Trump knows that he will not be able to speak as freely as before. Speaking freely, uttering vulgarities and absurdities, was in a certain

sense the source of his power, his false novelty. But now, with all the trappings of government, administration, the military, the economists, the bankers, the congress, including those in his own camp, it will be another story. And on election night we saw Trump change from one musical style to another, from one kind of theater to another. And he wasn't as good on the new stage as on the old one: he didn't sing as loudly; he was less "novel." That said, we do not know what margin of maneuvering this type of character will have once he becomes president of the United States. What we know for sure is that he is a symbol of the decomposition of the traditional political oligarchy and the birth of the figure of a new fascism, whose future is uncertain but which, in any case, is definitely not a good thing for the people who will have to endure it. This is the second term.

3 We therefore also have popular frustration, the feeling of a vague disorder, the fear of the future, the experience of being stuck in a dead end – all of this within a fraction of the middle class, but especially among the poor, among those who live in the provinces, the countless peasants of many regions of the world, the workers

without work . . . in short, the whole part of the world's population that has been reduced by the brutality of contemporary capitalism to invisibility and obscurity, without money and without any sense of orientation for their own existence. And this point is very important in the general situation of the world today: the lack of orientation, of stability, the feeling that their world has been destroyed without being replaced by another one in which they could come back to life. This is a sort of senseless destruction.

4 Finally, we are faced with the total absence of a political strategy, of another path. This is the particular oppression inflicted by what is sometimes called "the politics of no alternative," which put an end to the great historical hope for a just society, a hope that remained steadfast from 1792 to 1976. To be sure, there are many local political experiments. I am not saying that nothing exists in the way of a politics genuinely different from that which is dominating us. We all know that there are revolts, new occupations of squares in big cities, new mobilizations, a new ecological activism, etc. The point is not that there is a total absence

of any form of resistance or revolt. But there is the lack of another strategic path, of a conviction that could have the same power as the resigned belief according to which capitalism is the only possible path for the future of humanity as a whole. This is the lack of what I call an Idea, a great Idea. Only this great Idea could create the possibility of a unification, a strategic and global unification, of all the forms of resistance and political invention. Only this Idea could mediate between the individual subject and the collective and political task of communist emancipation. And only this Idea could also make possible an action gathering together very different subjectivities under the clear power of a shared idea.

The four terms of this inevitable dialectic that impels the history of the world today are thus the following: the strategic domination of global capitalism, the decomposition of the traditional bourgeois political oligarchy, the disarray and frustration of the peoples, and the lack of another strategic orientation, the weakness – let's just say the word – of the communist hypothesis. These four facts make up the crisis of the contemporary world. This crisis cannot be reduced to the economic crisis that began in 2007. It is much more a crisis of subjectivity, because, in the context of the four terms, the historical destiny of the human species is less and less clear.

* * *

So it is time to ask Lenin's famous question: "What is to be done?"

As far as Trump's election is concerned, I think we must first say that a reason for the success of this shady character is that the real contradiction today, the most important one, cannot take place between two forms of the same world. It cannot be inherent in the one and only path that has been imposed on us – that of global capitalism, of imperialist wars, and of the lack of any idea concerning the historical destiny of the human species.

I know that Hillary Clinton and Donald Trump are very different. The former comes from the heart of the classic establishment, while the latter comes from the fringe of the reactionary party. She was a cabinet official of Obama, for whom Trump has a kind of racist hatred. Yes, the traditional bourgeois oligarch and the fascisto-democratic parvenu are different, and I understand how, in the end, one might prefer her to him. However, we must not forget that this difference is located inside the same world, that it by no means expresses two visions of the world, two fundamentally distinct political strategies. And I think the success of Trump was possible only because the real contradiction in today's world, the true opposition between two antagonistic visions, could in no way be symbolized by the choice between Hillary Clinton and Donald Trump. Because, to tell you the truth, Hillary Clinton and Donald Trump, however different their styles may be, both belong to the small worldwide oligarchy that is capitalizing its profits on a worldwide scale.

In fact, during the primaries, during the whole phase leading up to the presidential election in the United States, the real contradiction expressed itself, in however attenuated a fashion (but let us not expect too much from public opinion in the great dominant power at the very center of the monster), between Trump and Bernie Sanders. All sorts of objections can be made to this statement. One might say that Trump, as a fascisto-democrat, is too outlandish to be a suitable representative of almighty capital. One might say that Bernie Sanders represents rather feebly the possibility of another strategic path, and that he is quite far from being a communist for a new era. One might observe that, by the time of the general election, Bernie Sanders had to support Hillary Clinton, whether he liked it or not. Granted. But we are in the belly of the beast, and in this place, at the level of symbolization, which is so important, the real contradiction in our world was much better represented by the opposition between Trump and Sanders than by the tandem Trump–Clinton. In Sanders's speeches and in his proposals, we can find several points that go beyond the demands of the world as it is, that deviate somewhat from the one and only path. There is nothing of the kind in Hillary Clinton's proposals.

Here we have a lesson in dialectics, a lesson in the different forms of contradiction. The contradiction between Hillary Clinton and Donald Trump, however intense, was nonetheless a relative rather than an absolute contradiction, a contradiction within the same parameters. The contradiction between Trump and Sanders was at least the possible beginning of a vision of the world that might go beyond the one that is imposed on us. Trump was on the side of a pseudo-popular subjectivity, reactive and obscure. Sanders was on the side of an active and enlightened popular subjectivity which seeks to orient itself, beyond the constraints of the one and only path, towards possible modes of being outside the monster. To be sure, this possible exteriority was murky and tepid, but it represented a courage that can be useful in looking for and finding the practical experience of another path.

We can say that the result of the elections in the United States is of a conservative nature, not so much because Trump and the reactionaries of the Republican Party emerged victorious as because it is the result of a secondary contradiction presented as if it were primary. Consequently, this election – and many others to come in many other countries – demands that we assess the situation in an absolutely innovative way. We can no longer content ourselves with people like Hillary Clinton, or with anything of the kind. We must create a return, if possible, towards a true contradiction. This is the lesson to be drawn from the horrible thing that happened yesterday in the "deep night." The task, now, is to construct a political orientation that would go well beyond the laws of the world as it is, even if the risk is that, initially, things may not be clear, and may even seem impossible. This is the moment to remember Lacan's formula "The real is the impossible." We must return to the real contradiction between politics in the service of capitalism and politics in the service of the peoples.

After Trump, we can no longer just keep on going. We must begin something new. It is not enough to criticize, to deny, to resist. Our task is to affirm a new beginning. And the first imperative is to affirm the existence of, and thus to make exist in public opinion, a fundamental strategic choice between two orientations, which, for my part, I would call – although there can be other words – the capitalist orientation and the communist orientation. We must return to what lay at the basis of the great political movements of the nineteenth century and during the first three quarters of the twentieth century, and whose central point is the making in-common (hence the word "communism") of everything concerning the great processes of production and exchange. And, for this to happen, we must allow for the dictatorship of private property and the pursuit of maximum profits for a minuscule minority of people to be abolished in a very large number of sectors.

Preparing the ground for this new beginning, leaving the counter-revolution that has been dominating us for the last forty years, creating the conditions for a return to a fundamental choice between two paths – all this is the true essence of politics today. When there is only one path, only one strategic orientation, politics, in reality, gradually disappears. Trump is the symbol of this sort of disappearance. What are Trump's "politics"? Nobody knows, for Trump is a figure, a character, rather than a politics. The return of politics is the return to the existence of a fundamental choice.

In sum, at the level of philosophical generality, we can say this: the essential political gesture, today, is the return of dialectics, which is to say, the return to the real Two, beyond the deceptive One. On every issue, we must be the shrewd and tenacious activists of this return.

Two Weeks after the Election of Trump

Tufts University, Boston

What I'd like to do this evening is to provoke some philosophical meditations on the election of Trump. In itself, the election of Trump is not a great philosophical event. But it's a very interesting fact on many levels. Is the election of Trump a true disaster, the beginning of the end of democratic freedom, the triumph of racism, sexism, and social violence? Certainly it is a dark day for freedom, justice, and equality. I understand that, on the level of public opinion, many people feel anxious and depressed, that they are afraid for the future of the United States and finally of the world itself. I understand too that they are angry, that they oppose everything that the new president represents for them: violence, vulgarity, corruption, and contempt for the difficult lives of millions of people. I am on the side of revolts in the streets by thousands of young men and women. But, in some sense, we must affirm that Donald Trump in himself is something obscure and not really interesting. We must get beyond our anxiety and reach a point of calm, of determination, of lucidity. After all, Trump is like a blemish on the face of the contemporary political world. Trump must be interpreted as an ugly symptom of the global situation, not only of the United States but of the world, the world in which we are living today. So I propose to take the election of Donald Trump as the point of departure for a meditation concerning our living world today. I propose, if you like, to reconstruct Trump as a philosophical category – which is a strong transformation. I propose to construct Trump in three stages: first, the global situation of the contemporary world; second, the political crisis of what is called "democracy" – that is, a form of state power in the Western world, the world of which the United States, Europe, and Japan are the centre; and, third, the choices with which we are confronted, the answer to the old question: now that Trump is in power, what is to be done?

* * *

(I, 1) First, the overall situation of today is in fact – it's obvious, but we must emphasize the point – a complete victory of globalized capitalism. This has many implications. First, monstrous inequalities, of which I offer only one example: today, 264 people have the same amount of money as a total of 7 billion other people. It's probably the most important difference in the situation of humanity since the beginning of humanity's existence. The difference is much greater than during the times of aristocratic power and absolute monarchy. It's a real difference, since it results in two completely different worlds, two completely different visions of life itself; as you know, moreover, the fundamental law of capitalism, namely the process of capital's concentration, operates at an accelerated pace today. So maybe tomorrow it will be not 264 people but only two or three. We would have a sort of financial democracy transformed into a financial kingdom. This is the first point, and it is very important, because it is not entirely visible from the perspective of the West. It's an obvious truth, however, in Africa, in Asia, in Latin America, even if it's not completely obvious here. But if we want to understand the situation here, we must understand the situation of the world as a whole. It's a mistake to examine only our situation without thinking about the relationship between it and the situation of the world as a whole.

(I, 2) The second point: what is the "contemporary subject"? What is the human being of today? What are the possible choices of a contemporary subject? I think that the contemporary subject has in fact four possibilities in today's globalized capitalism. The first is to be an owner, a landlord, a capitalist. The second is to be at once an employee and a consumer – that is, to sell your labour and to buy commodities; to be in the labour market, on the one hand, and in the great marketplace of products, on the other. So the contemporary subject is between two markets, the market of labour, of jobs, and the market of products. This second position is that of many millions of people today. The third possibility is to be a poor peasant, a truly poor peasant, in Africa for example, perched at the limit of existence, of the very possibility of life. And the forth possibility is to be nothing at all, neither a consumer nor an employee nor a peasant nor a capitalist. Probably 3 billion people today are in that position, and they are wandering through the world, searching for a place to live. This point is about the distribution of subjectivities and about how people live today; we must see this point clearly.

(I, 3) The third point, which is the consequence of the previous two, is that the unity of all this, what constitutes it as a world in some sense, is in fact money. It's the circulation of money that is the true definition of this world. This is the fundamental point to be derived from the monstrous unity of all these contradictory determinations. And the point is probably very important today, although I can agree to call it a hypothesis: it's a major challenge to understand why, on the one hand, you have so many people without jobs who are wandering through the world trying to find work while, on the other, you have long working weeks for all the people who do have jobs. It would be reasonable to create a working week that would be appropriate to this situation. But that's not what has happened. In my country, many presidential candidates are proposing to lengthen the working week, from 35 hours to 40 hours. And we have 10 percent of the population in France – not in Africa or in Asia – who are without jobs and who are wandering through the country trying to find something to do. And so, probably, capitalism itself at this point is not able to provide the totality of the world's population with jobs. What we have here is a sort of limit of the capitalist possibility. Capitalism is incapable of producing jobs for everyone because, as you know, capitalists give work to people only if they expect to make a profit. It's a complex but obvious law of capitalism that profit is linked to the working week: you must have a long working week to make a profit. So maybe the most important point in the world today is that this enormous mass of wandering people searching for a place to live cannot be forced under the domination of globalized capitalism. In other words, from the perspective of globalized capitalism itself, we have today a surplus of humanity – a surplus of people without any destination, without any reason to exist.

(I, 4) Another point of a different nature concerning the global situation today is the constant affirmation that there exists only one way, only one future – namely, the continuation of globalized capitalism. There can be no global idea that affirms the possibility of something else. It is quite striking that the very nature of propaganda today is not to say that capitalism is a great thing: it suffices to say that there exists no other possibility. In fact, capitalism is the first social organization in which it is possible to say that this organization is very bad; making that statement has no consequences. In the old world, for example in monarchy, we were not allowed to say that the king is horrible; the stability of the world implied that we must be in favour of the world as it is; this subjectivity is really a subjectivity of faith in the world as it is. This is not the case in capitalism. In capitalism, it is sufficient to say that nothing else is possible. It was the position of Churchill himself, who said "it's not a good system, but it's the best" – the best, with the possibility that it could be still very bad. And so the nonexistence of another way, another strategy for the life of humanity as such, is a very important point today; it's a world that is very different from the world before, because another way existed between 1917 (that is, the Russian Revolution) and the beginning of the

1980s. Naturally, we must discuss the validity of this other way – that's another problem – but you have two possibilities, both on a global scale. There could be many discussions concerning these two possibilities and the relationship between them; it might be asked whether the communist hypothesis is really acceptable, and so on. But there existed two possibilities, and the great victory of globalized capitalism has been to suppress the existence of these two possibilities, not just to bring about the dissolution and disappearance of the socialist states, the end of both the Soviet Union and Maoist China. These have been concrete empirical victories. But the ideological victory is much more important: this is the victory of the conviction that, "OK, capitalism is not good, monstrous inequalities are horrible, and so on, but there is no other possibility," and so this reduction from two to one is a very fundamental fact in recent history. We are, in some sense, in a consensus – a negative consensus, not an *enthousiasme général* for capitalism, but capitalism doesn't demand that sort of thing. This consensus is the negative idea that nothing else is possible, and therefore that only some local transformations on minor points are possible, but that the global system cannot be changed.

All this composes the general vision of the world as it is, and in some sense Trump is a symptom.

* * *

(II) My second point is that the world as it is produces different symptoms in the political field: the world as it is creates a political crisis, a profound political crisis concerning the definitions of politics itself, of democracy, of the state, of government, and finally of the necessity of government. I want to explain why. And, to make it clearer, I will try to represent this situation in the form of a picture [see figure 1]. Suppose this surface [the background to figure 1] is the entire world, the infinity of the historical world of today: modern politics always begins with the idea that this world is not completely unified but divided into two parts. We observe in fact that the democratic system is always a system in which we have – we must have – two different tendencies as a minimum; if you have only one tendency, it's not a democratic system, because there is no choice. So the idea of choice is the

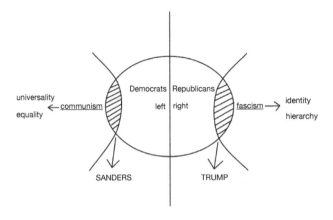

Figure 1

idea that there is a reason to have two different
political parties, two different orientations – a
division of the subjective world between two
different global tendencies. In some sense, if we
observe the history of all this, we see that, on
one side, we have a tendency in the direction
of universality and equality and, on the other, a
tendency to identity und hierarchy. That is the
most abstract distinction between the left and
the right, between Democrats and Republicans,
between communists and capitalists, and so on.
There are many names, many different histories,
many incarnations of all this: the subjective state

35

occurs within the polarization between the two tendencies.

The global democratic system – that is, the constitutional system in our world, the system with elections, representation, and so on – is the idea that the two dispositions, the two parts of the world, can be represented by organizations or parties or factions; that there is a process of representation of this subjective differentiation, this subjective contradiction, which is ultimately the power of the state. By the mediation of the parties, the power of the state is distributed, sometimes divided, between the different tendencies. So we can describe the global representation as such. What is named today the "political elite" or "professional politicians" represents the tension between the two tendencies at the center of the general space in the form of two different organizations or parties. So we can have, for example, Democrats and Republicans, we can also have left and right, and so on.

The fundamental characteristic of this sort of system is that, in some sense, the division cannot be too strong, because if the division at the level of the state is too strong we have civil war. So the very essence of this sort of political system is to represent the contradiction without opening up the possibility of civil war. In the United States, you are very familiar with such a division in the form of the Civil War – a terrible war, because it was impossible to create a state where you have on one side [the right side of figure 1] the possibility of slavery and on other [the left side of figure 1] the impossibility of slavery. So the war between the South and the North was the moment when the unified representation of the fundamental contradiction was impossible. So, in order to avoid a civil war, we must have a sort of common opinion among the political elite. But what, in the end, is this common opinion? In the world as it is, the common opinion is precisely that the general law of the space as a whole [which is represented by the background to figure 1] is globalized capitalism. So there really is something like a common ideology, which creates a formal unity of global representation at the level of the state and which excludes civil war at the price of accepting the general law as the structure of the world as it is – the law, in short, of globalized capitalism.

Of course, this complicity between the two parties, which is the key to the existence of the state, is criticized by many groups. So we have, on both sides, organizations, groups, ideologies, and individuals, some of whom are saying, "No, this political elite is not sufficiently on the side of universality and equality," while others are saying, "No, it's not sufficiently on the side of identity, hierarchy, and old ideas." So we have something like the permanent possibility that there exists something on the left of the left and something on the right of the right. We know very well that, in the previous sequence, the limit of this extension of representation on the left was communism and the limit on the other side was fascism. So communism and fascism were outside the system of representation because they constituted the limits of the tension between the two fundamental polarities; but, at the same time, they always had points of intersection with the global elite. For example, the Communist Party in France has had representatives in the National Assembly, and eventually, in 1981, they entered the government. And, after that, they were as good as dead, because to be in government was in fact contradictory to their proper existence, which was precisely to criticize the classical representation. On the other side, the same thing happens with fascism. Fascism is by itself out-side of the normal representation in democracy, but sometimes fascism is also inside the govern-ment and can take power. This was the case in Germany just before the Second World War, for example.

So we have a very complex relationship between two contradictions: the fundamental contradiction, latent at the global level, between communism and fascism (these were their names during the 1930s, but they can have other names); and the contradiction, accepted at the level of the state, between left and right, Democratic and Republican – a contradiction that is by neces-sity, I am arguing, a weak contradiction. Between fascism and communism we have a true contra-diction, a contradiction without any possible reconciliation. At the center of the state we have a weak contradiction dominated by the common idea that the global structure cannot be changed.

This system, which is the general system in our countries, cannot exist when the tensions between the two polarities become too strong, because, if the external tension on the two sides is really strong, it's very difficult to maintain the complic-ity between the two central parties. And I think we can see symptoms that something like this is happening today in the fact that, at the global level, capitalism cannot really satisfy all the interests involved in the global situation. And so, what happens? What happens is that too many people are saying that the official left is weak compared to the right. And, on the other side, too many people are saying that the representation of their interests by Republicans or by the right is too weak. And so all this creates the possibility of a disjunction of the state itself. If Democrats or the left are too violently attached to their values or if, on the other hand, Republicans or the right are also too attached to their contradictory values, the unity of the state is not easy to maintain.

So, Trump is here [see figure 1]. Trump is at the intersection between the official representation and what exceeds it. He is in the Republican Party, but he also represents something outside it: sexism, racism, tendencies towards fascism. In some sense, with much greater sophistication, Bernie Sanders is on the other side. And so we can say something like this: the true contradiction during your last election was not really between Hillary Clinton, who is here [in the place on the board where it says "Democrats"], and Trump, who is here [TRUMP]. The true contradiction, the latent true contradiction, was between Bernie Sanders and Trump. What was significant in the election was the contradiction between Bernie Sanders and Trump and not the contradiction between Hillary Clinton, who is a perfect representation of the classic old Democratic Party in its function of complicity with the elite and global capitalism. And in my opinion this is why, at the end of the day, Trump won: he was on the side of the true contradiction. In the lack of symmetry between Hillary Clinton and Trump, Trump was finally in the stronger position, even though he did not win the popular vote. But the real reason for his success is the lack of symmetry in the contradiction between him and Clinton in a sequence where ultimately the system itself is in crisis. That is my descriptive point concerning the political facts today.

We can sum all this up by saying that, in the democratic system, there are three historical possibilities. (1) There is a normal possibility, according to which the contradiction between the left elite and the right elite functions normally, so that their complicity is sufficient to maintain the unity of the state at its normal level. Here, the global subjective contradiction is represented by the central complicity without too much difficulty. It's the law of the system, the normal existence of the system. (2) There is the possibility of crisis, when the true contradiction is not really normal. For example, in France today, we have no normal contradiction at the level of the state, because the left is practically dead and so everything is decided inside the right itself. But if the decisions are made inside the right, the system is not normal: it's in a crisis. This is the second form, when the election is not organized by the true contradiction from the point of view of the people. People don't think that it's the true contradiction. (3) And there is a third possibility, which is when finally the crisis is so strong that you have a real conflict. This is a conflict between the fundamental tendencies, a conflict between fascism and communism (among other possible names), but a conflict which raises the possibility of civil war. And so perhaps, today, the democratic system everywhere in the world, not only here in the United States, is moving from two dispositions – two big parties and their respective alternatives – to four dispositions. In other words, we have not only these two [Republicans

42

and Democrats], but also two other differences [Trump and Sanders, corresponding to the true contradiction between fascism and communism, their respective representational versions in the middle being Republicans and Democrats]. And when we have four different possibilities and not two, it's a crisis of what? A crisis of the political elite, because the political elite is precisely the product of the normal functionality – that is, of the normal existence – of the center of the state.

And finally there appears a symptom: in France, the great symptom is that people can't distinguish practically between the left and the right; François Hollande is a political blob. Here, the crisis is such that people ended up choosing Trump and not the regular Republicans. And so it's not the true contradiction. The symptom of the crisis is the appearance of strange persons who are very difficult to understand: they are politicians, but they are in some sense like new gangsters. This was the case with Berlusconi in Italy. Berlusconi was the first to represent the victory within the democratic system of some-body who was openly a gangster and with the same characteristics as Trump: vulgarity, sexism, complete contempt for intellectuals, and so on.

And Nicolas Sarkozy was not unlike this gangster figure. I've said on one of the French television channels that Sarkozy is a *voyou*, a thug. It's not a political category. But the point is that all these guys are not politicians in the sense of the ordinary political elite. They are coming from outside. And I think, ultimately, the fundamental symptom today is the inability of the two big parties to continue their mixture of contradiction and collaboration. That is the point; that is the difficulty. Everything is normal if there is simultaneously contradiction and collaboration, which preserves the unity of the state. And I think this crisis is a result of the global situation of capitalism, of the inability of global capitalism to solve the problems of all the people existing in our countries. And so we really have some hard contradictions in the world as it is, with the existence of billions of people wandering and searching for a place to live. As a result, the normal collaboration – or quasi-collaboration – of two parties at the apex of the state becomes more and more difficult.

To summarize: we must take into consideration four terms, I think, to understand all this. It's a recapitulation of what I call the crisis of today:

1 the brutality and the blind violence of contemporary capitalism, the return to the brutality and blind violence of capitalism for most of the nineteenth century. Read Dickens! We are returning to a new form of the Dickensian age . . .;

2 the decomposition of the political elite – this whole story [which you can see in figure 1] – raising the possibility of a new fascism, a very dark result;

3 popular frustration in the face of all this, the feeling of an obscure disorder, the conviction that there is no acceptable orientation of the world, that I can't go on, but – to echo Beckett at the end of one of his famous books – capitalism can't go on, so it goes on;

4 and, finally, the lack of another strategic way.

So, in an arithmetical formalization, we might say: at the global level we have the passage from two strategic ways – the contradiction of capitalism and communism – to one – globalized capitalism as the only strategic way – and at the level of politics we pass from two to four. But among these four there are inequalities; for the moment the greatest strength is on the right side.

The possibility of a new form of fascism is really present. And the lack, the terrible lack, is the lack of something on the other side. We will return to this point.

*   *   *

(III) What I call the crisis of today is the system of these four points. So what is our task? What is to be done? I think that we must absolutely find something on the side of universality and equality; we have to create something new. We cannot repeat; we have to invent. My proposal at the philosophical level is to adopt the name that has symbolized this polarity for a whole century, which is the word "communism." To be sure, it's a word that is fundamentally histor-ically corrupted and difficult. I know this, but in some sense the same is true for "democracy": democracy has been largely the organization, on a large scale, of imperialism, colonialism, and a general complicity with the development of monstrous inequalities, with the idea that capitalism is the only possible strategic way. In some sense, all political words are corrupted. History is a great corruption of everything that is present in history itself. But a name is only a name. What we lack is an Idea, a great Idea. What do I call an idea? It's a philosophical term, a mediation between individual subjects and the collective and political task, movement, or organization. An idea is the possibility of action across and with very different subjectivities. An idea is the possibility that very different subjectivities, very different social positions, very different nationalities, work in a common movement under the same concept. And I think that we can summarize this idea in some very simple points, which in fact have been the points of communism. But we can't repeat them in their primitive form.

The first point is that it is not a necessity for social organization to reside in private property and monstrous inequalities. This point is very important, because the propaganda of capitalism is precisely to say that it is a necessity: "We cannot do anything else. We have the historical proof of the failure of communism and so we must return to the good old idea that private property must be the key to development and social organization." This point is always a displacement of the global system in the direction of the right, and even Trump is a consequence of this situation, a situation without any answering vision on the other side. And so we must first affirm that it is not a necessity; we must resist the conviction that the only possibility is globalized capitalism. We have to pass from one to two. We must return absolutely to the conviction that there exist two strategic ways and not one. And we can organize limited experiences that demonstrate that it is not a necessity, that you can organize production and social life in a form that is not the dictatorship of private property. And so finally we can affirm that it is not true that private property and monstrous inequalities must forever be the law of the becoming of humanity.

The second point is that it is not a necessity that human work should be divided between such noble activities as intellectual creation and government, on the one hand, and manual labor and common material existence, on the other. So the specialization of labour is not an internal law. This is a very important point. The opposition between intellectual work and manual work must be undone in the long term; we must bring about a reconciliation of humanity at the level of work, at the level of what is done day after day, and not only at the top.

The third principle is that it's not a necessity for human beings – and this point goes against the right – to be separated by national, racial, religious, or sexual boundaries. Equality must exist across differences, and difference must not be an obstacle to equality. It is a philosophical argument of the right that equality is impossible because there are too many differences among human beings. "Naturally," they say, "some are intelligent and some are stupid," and so on. So the fight against equality is always on the side of identities: "your identity is to be a poor man and stupid," or "your identity is to be a rich man and intelligent," or "you are white and good," or "you are black and bad." So there is a close relationship between the cult of identities and the opposition to equality. But we must affirm philosophically, as a dialectical position, that equality must exist across differences and thus that differences are not obstacles to equality. Equality must be a dialectics of difference itself. The creative capacity of difference is equality. We must reject the belief that, in the name of differences, equality is impossible. So, to put it concretely: boundaries, refusal of the other in any form, all this must disappear. It is not in any way a natural law.

And the last principle is that there is no necessity for a state in the form of a separated and armed power. We can go in the direction of what Marx calls "free association" – that is, the idea that everything concerning people's lives and futures can be discussed appropriately in meetings among people themselves.

So these four points can be summarized easily: collectivism against private property, polymorphous work against specialization, concrete universalism against closed identities, and free association against the state. I would emphasize that these are only principles, not really a concrete program; but with these principles we can judge all political programs, decisions, parties, and ideas. Take a decision, by the government or by other authorities: the question will be: "Is this decision moving in the direction of the four principles or not?" The principles are the protocol of judgment concerning all decisions, ideas, and proposals in the field of politics. If a decision, or a proposal, is in the direction of the four principles, we can say it's a good one; we can determine whether or not it is possible, and so on. If it's clearly against the principles, it's a bad decision, a bad idea, a bad program. So we can have in the new strategic vision a principle of judgment in the political field and in the construction of the new strategic project. This principle of judgment makes possible a true vision of the new strategic direction of humanity as such.

I return to the concrete situation. At one point, Bernie Sanders seemed to propose something like a new political group under the name "Our Revolution." It seems to me that he has more recently made the choice to return to the games and compromises of the Democratic Party. Let me just say, as I begin to conclude: I might be able to trust him in the first direction, but certainly not in the second.

I began with the success of Trump; I end with the success of Trump. The success of Trump, understood as a symptom, must open up a new opportunity for the idea inherent in the words "our revolution." With the four principles we have an approximate idea, at the level of judgment, of the possibility of something like this. Today, against what Trump symbolizes – reaction, ideological violence, the imperialist decomposition of the political system – why not say, "OK, Our Revolution"? But we must be clear about the words. "Revolution" must be understood as a process in accord with the four principles. And we can check to make sure that what is proposed is moving in that direction. And "our" – what is "our"? "Our" in one sense can mean: in relationship with a strong alliance; "our" is not everybody. It's not Trump, for example. It's a strong alliance, probably among some intellectuals, a large contingent of young people, and what we might call the "nomadic proletariat" of today, the workers and the unemployed who are everywhere. If we have something like this alliance of intellectuals, the young, and the nomadic workers of the world on one side, and if we have, informing this alliance, the four principles, we can have hope. This is the sort of thing that we must invent and create. The system cannot propose a place for novelty. So we must create something outside the system as it is. [In figure 1], the left is the limit of the system.

It's very difficult. It's very difficult today, I know, but probably after Trump we must say to ourselves: "Only one world and only one courage." Thank you.

Questions

Q1: My question pertains to those of us who are interested in promoting a Maoist politics today in the United States. We are obviously a long distance from anything worthy of the name of a "party," but starting in the late 1980s you and your comrades began to speak of "politics without a party in which the political organization is orientated towards the prescriptive," but in your recent introduction to the French translation of Hongsheng Jiang's dissertation on the Paris Commune in Shanghai you were saying that you could call the political organization a party. I was wondering if you could elaborate on this a little bit more. I'm specifically curious about your objection to the party that is oriented towards representing the interest of a class and how that impedes the ability of a party to identify the principal contradictions and the principal aspect of a contradiction in a given situation.

Badiou: Yes, the question is in fact a central question in the political field today. And why? Because the experience demonstrates that to have a real new strategic view we must always discuss three terms. There is the question of power, which is the stable element in history. In any case we have something like a state. And all the forms of politics are confronted with the question of the state, the question of power. This is the first term.

On the other hand we have big mass movements, revolts, spontaneous expressions of the ideas of people, and it's a necessary part of new politics. Without movements we can't affirm that a new politics exists, naturally. Movement, revolt, and so on, are indispensable to the possibility of constructing a new strategy or a new strain, naturally. But the problem is that between the state and the movements there must be something else. Why? For a very important reason, which is that the state always has time on its side. The state can continue. The state is the continuity of the power. And the movement is not continuous. The movement is always a sequence. All movements begin and end. So there is a lack of symmetry between the power and the movement which is fundamentally a lack of symmetry at the level of time. And you know the classical disappointment when the movement finishes. The people cannot be eternally in the movement because they have to return to their families, jobs, work, and so on. They can't be forever in the delicious feeling of revolt and movement. And the state is for a good reason called the "state."

Patience is on the side of the state. The state must continue. And the state will be there after the movement, always. So it's a political necessity that, on the side of the new strategy, some new terms, some figures, sometimes account for the duration, account for the time of the new politics. The name of this term is "organization." And we cannot escape the question of organization, because organization is the memory of the movement. It's the idea of the movement in the duration of time. It's the possibility to be not only in the necessary radicality of the movement but to have time to construct the new strategy and maybe also to be stronger in the next movement. "What is an organization?" is in the end the most difficult problem today, the question of what exactly are the problems which can be solved only by an organization.

The Leninist organization, the classical Communist Party, was created by Lenin to solve a precise problem, a very precise problem. This problem was: "How can we be victorious?", because during the whole of the nineteenth century all the big revolts of workers – the Commune de Paris, May '48, and so on – were bloodily crushed. And so at the end of the nineteenth century the question was not the question of movement, because we had many experiences of substantial insurrections of workers, but the question was to be victorious. We cannot continue in the way of constant defeat and dispersion. And we cannot accept what the social democratic parties in Germany or in France did – that is, finally to reduce the action to this place [the inner circle on figure 1], the place of collaboration. So the question of organization, at the beginning of the last century, was clearly not an organization to occupy the place of collaboration – in government, parliament, and so on – nor was it the pure anarchy which led in the end to the bloody massacre of thousands of workers in the streets of Paris. And Lenin proposed a strictly disciplined organization, in some sense in the military model, an organization which is able to continue the action not only in the context of the movement but also in the face of the state, maybe an organization which is able to seize power, to destroy the power of the enemy. So the Leninist organization solved one problem, the problem of victory. And Lenin himself said: "We are in the century of victorious revolutions." It was the idea that the nineteenth century was the century of the invention of the communist revolution, but it failed in regard to the question of power. And Lenin had the idea that we are in the century of victory of revolution, and that was why the Leninist vision was actually accepted by millions of people for many years. It was in the idea of victory – in some sense the first victory of pure workers, and so on, in the history of humanity. So it was really an event, an extraordinary event. What we might very well observe in terms of historical destiny is that the party, the classical party made to be victorious, is certainly victorious under particular circumstances – it was the case in Russia and in China too, after the Second World War – but that it has difficulties in organizing a new society. Power is one thing, but the function of power is to continue the new strategy and not to be only power as such. And so the big problem has been: "How can we continue in the direction of communism with this type of party which is appropriate to victory, but which has difficulties conserving the dynamic of the action when it is in power and which maybe can be finally transformed into a new figure of state oppression?" After that we have many ideas and attempts to transform the Leninist vision of the party and all that under the idea that we must have some form of organization which is between the movement and the state, but which must not be confused with the state. So we must invent not only the possibility of seizing power but the possibility of being organized outside power even if you are in power – and so to create organizations which are not confused with power, with the state, and will really represent the ideas of the movement. And the movement must continue, revolt; the movement, mobilization of masses must continue even under socialist power. But now this invention is not realized completely. It was the failure of the Cultural Revolution in China; in some sense, it has been the failure, the historical failure, of that sort of perspective. And so we must certainly open the question of organization in the sense of some organization that must stay near the movement, with the idea of the movement and which controls the state, which has the power to control the state, to exercise a sort of popular dictatorship over the state. So the idea is not to create the dictatorship of the state over the people but the dictatorship of people over the state. It's our future, courageously.

Q2:   I have two points, one is concerning the global situation, the global market and the other is more concerning the USA.

Do you think that we are moving towards a third world war because the contradictions, the polarities, concerning the global market are so big that a big conflict on an international level at some point can't be avoided?

My second point concerns the United States more internally: I think a problem of the Marxist analysis is that it has always avoided the question of race. If you look, for example, at what happened in the USA in the 1960s, particularly after the Voting Rights Act of 1965, you see that the violence against blacks was increasing and also the number of people who joined the Ku Klux Klan was increasing during that time. So, even if black people obtained more rights, there is a reactionary tendency which creates a tension inside the state because the white ultra-right is getting stronger.

Badiou: Yes, about your first question I am not totally optimistic in fact. I think that today a global war, probably with Africa at the center of ambitions and conflicts between forces, is really possible. And, you know, there has been always a dialectics between war and revolutions. Lenin used to say – first hypothesis – the revolution creates a situation where war is impossible. Second hypothesis: war provokes the revolution. And I think that, right now, we don't believe in the first hypothesis. There is no historical situation where revolution, in some sense, creates the impossibility of war. The revolutionary power existed when the Second World War broke out, and so on. So it's really a possibility, and it's also a possibility that the dynamic of global capitalism today is moving towards a war. If the problem of capitalism is the impossibility of suppressing the surplus of humanity – about which I have spoken – that is, the existence of billions of human beings who have no significance for capitalism itself – because that is the present vision, many of them in Africa, a lot of them in Africa. Maybe a solution would be a big war, because a big war is a simplistic solution to a demographic problem. And so we should also keep in mind that, in order to escape the risk of a big war, it is also necessary to create a new political strategy. Because the law of the capitalism of today is not to escape war but much more to provoke in the end a big planetary conflict.

To the second point: it's true that the question of identities, the question of race and of racism, and so on, has been a weakness of classical Marxism. Classical Marxism has been on the side of universalism without making a precise attempt to observe the questions of identity as such. I think that we should affirm now, after all this experience, that it is very important that there is no contradiction between political universalism and the existence of differences and that the existence of differences must be protected in the name of universalism itself. It's a philosophical question, in some sense, which is not so easy to answer: what is the real relationship between the ideal of universality – which is the affirmation that in the end there is one humanity and that all human beings are equal – and the real existence of different identities? And the solution to the problem is a dialectical one, and that is the fact that equality is not against the existence of symbolic identities but goes across the differences and along with the differences, in the complete recognition of differences. Ultimately we can define politics as such as something which is on the side of universality with acceptance of all figures of identity without making identities an obstacle to equality and universalism. That is the definition of the new strategic politics.

And about my first remark to your question: there is finally a relationship between the question of war and the question of identities. I observe that today, in France for example, there is a sort of affirmation of war against Islam that is, after all, a war against a form of identity. And so in the history of human beings practically all wars have been made in the name of identities, national identities, racial identities. And today our government is speaking of war between "civilized" people and "barbarian" people – massive identities too. Very often when the political affirmation is the identity-affirmation, not in dialectic with universality but by itself, war is a strong possibility.

Q3: In your talk you moved very quickly from the election of Trump to these broader and, I think, very familiar ideas about the evils of global capitalism, the left–right divide, and so on. But I wonder if one has to be a bit more careful about doing that, because of course what's interesting and fascinating and terrifying about Trump is the way that he scrambles many of these familiar categories and oppositions. So I think one could contest pretty much everything that you have on the board there, certainly where you place Trump. Now, of course, one of the problems of talking about Trump is: who knows what he really believes? But one thing we do know is that he has been hostile to free trade for a very long time. I lived in New York City in the late 1980s and early 1990s, and often you would read about Trump railing against free trade in the popular press, and he has continued to do so ever since. He views free trade as a zero-sum game, so if one country is winning another must be losing, and that has been a very constant theme in his work. Now who knows whether he's going to engage in trade wars, and so on. But his stance does suggest that you can't tie him quite so easily in the way that you do to the triumph of global capitalism, that he represents something quite different which is sometimes called economic nationalism or nationalist capitalism, but I think one must be a bit more careful in tying Trump to this idea and also to this very familiar left–right opposition. He is more interesting than that.

Badiou: You know, I interpret Trump precisely as a symptom of a crisis of globalized capitalism as a system, as a crisis of the political organization of the economic system. That is the point. Naturally, Trump, for example, proposes nationalist restrictions of universal trade, proposes to expel Mexican workers, and so on. And all that, in some sense, is not compatible with the sovereignty of the global market, it's true. But it's precisely a symptom that the relationship between the global existence of capitalism at the scale of the world, on the one hand, and the political system, on the other, which is, on the national scale, the state and so on, is in profound crisis. I think that the political elite today cannot propose to the people a correct articulation [of the contradictions] between their life and the global situation of the market. That is the point. And so the reason for the appearance of figures like Trump and Berlusconi and so on is that in some sense the political system today cannot control the effect of globalized capitalism. In some sense globalized capitalism cannot recognize states and nationalities and so on. It's not its problem. You know the 264 persons who are . . . they are internationalist, in some sense, they are in Shanghai, Chicago, São Paolo, and so on. The circulation of money is the unique principle of the system, but it cannot be the system of the state, of a national state. So today there is the contradiction of the political field and the economic organization. The political field stays at the level of the state and the global organization is not at the level of the state. And so we have reactive nationalism against this situation and we have no concrete universalism in the other sense, because true universality would be against the global market, naturally, and in the proposition of another form, a different form of organization, of the collaboration between people concerning production. And that is the situation. And so Trump, I agree with you, is a contradictory symptom at this time. He is a symptom of something which is wrong in the relationship of the appropriation of political power to the present existence of the global market. And it's normal in some sense, because in the end the global market cannot take into consideration the limit and the identity in the form of nationalism, and so on. In some sense it's an abstract power. It's the power of money. And this abstraction is an oppressive abstraction even in its effect on the mediation of this abstraction, which is the political elite in the United States or in France. This is the heart of the crisis, and this is why the political situation progressively becomes strange and dangerous and unstable, because in reality political power has no means to control, at the scale of the nation, the effects of globalized capitalism. And, for example, Trump says that he must organize an economic war against China, but in fact at the level of the global market there is a close relationship between the United States and China. It will be a disaster, in fact, this economic war. And so it's a real contradiction between two subjective perceptions of the situation. And this is why normally, when capitalism is at the end of its expansion, when we have really globalized capitalism, the only civilized situation is communism, because inside of capitalism itself we can't organize the community of human beings on a large scale. It is impossible, because we have inequalities that are too monstrous. We must absolutely destroy the dictatorship of private property. If it is not destroyed, you have this bloody contradiction in the long run between the life of people and the global system of organization of social relationships, and finally of the ordinary lives of people. And so it's true that after capitalism, at the end of capitalism, it's communism or barbarism, or complete barbarism. That is, in fact, atomic war.

66

Q4: Donald Trump has promised a huge number of things to his political base. It is maybe impossible for him to fulfil all those promises, particularly some of the more, let's say aggressive, red meat kind of things that he wants to do, like building a wall between Mexico and the United States. How do you think that his political base will react in case he fails to fulfil all his promises?

In this country as well as in other countries there is something which I, and others as well, would refer to as a "permanent government." In the USA this permanent government consists of the CIA, the NSA, the Pentagon, etc. Now, if Trump is successful in doing much of what he is proposing to do, if he creates as much disturbance as he seems to be wanting to create, is it not possible that the permanent government will just get rid of the guy?

Badiou: If they kill Trump, that's OK. It is true that Trump is in some sense much more of a problem than a solution for the state itself. I think something like that. It has always been the case that when there is a crisis in the political field there appear guys in the style of Berlusconi, Trump, and, finally, Mussolini or Hitler. Where is the difference? The difference is – and that is very important – in order to be a true and dangerous fascist, you have to construct your proper organization, your proper party. It's very decisive. Hitler and Mussolini *were* their parties. There were not parts of the Republicans or something like that. They had really strong organizations, militarized organizations which were able to kill, to destroy the enemies. So when the crisis is completely developed we must see the creation not only of some figures like Berlusconi or Trump but of new organizations which are separated from the system and which can seize power for themselves and not with the help of others. Naturally Trump is not in this position today, which is a blessing in a way. He is in the melting pot of the Republican elite, and he is more and more in a bad position, in some sense. If finally his end is a car accident, . . . well. It's not a necessity for the political elite. The most probable fate of Trump is to become weak, in fact, to become paralyzed in the face of many problems, and this is why I take Trump himself not for a very, very dangerous guy but as a symptom of a bad situation. And this is why we must look at the situation which created Trump and not be fascinated by Trump himself.